3

**Please return or renew by
latest date below**

LOANS MAY BE RENEWED BY PHONE

NOTES ON VISITATIONS
POEMS 1936–1975

GEORGE WOODCOCK

Anansi Toronto

Published with the assistance of the Canada Council and the
Ontario Arts Council by

House of Anansi Press Limited
35 Britain Street
Toronto, Canada.

ISBN: 0-88784-134-1.

HAP 33

Canadian Shared Cataloguing in Publication Data

   Woodcock, George, 1912—
     Notes on visitations.

   (House of Anansi poetry series ; HAP 33)
   Poems.
   ISBN 0-88784-134-1

   I. Title.

   PS8545.0745N6   811'.5'4
   PR9199.3.W

ACKNOWLEDGMENT

Some of these poems have appeared in earlier volumes, now out of print:
The White Island (Fortune Press),
The Centre Cannot Hold (Routledge & Kegan Paul),
Imagine the South (Untide Press),
Six Poems (Blue Moon Press),
and *Selected Poems* (Clarke, Irwin & Company Ltd.).

Others, hitherto uncollected, have appeared in *Malahat Review*, *Tamarack Review*, *Saturday Night* and *Canadian Forum*.

I am grateful to all these publishers and journals for their encouragement.

CONTENTS

INTRODUCTION

George Woodcock has written some dozens of books; I don't know how many. I have twenty of them, signed by him, in my bookcase. He's an authority on nearly everything: Bakunin, anarchism, Gabriel Dumont (you don't know who Dumont is?), Doukhobors, India, Gandhi, Orwell, Peru and McCleery Street in Vancouver. He writes books like other people breathe, and is a wise man, somewhat shy.

Woodcock is also the editor of Canadian Literature, *a sort of house organ for the stuff. In fact, in some not obscure sense, he is* Can Lit*—to the degree that a few universities in this country are now including it on their curriculum. Woodcock is the all-rounder, a literary and human person seemingly interested in and knowledgeable about everything. I don't mean that I think him infallible or any such silly quality: but if all this sounds like exaggeration, take a look at what the man has written.*

I've wondered occasionally how he does it, has the sheer vitality to write all those books. One big reason is Inge, his wife. She drives the Volks and he doesn't. She also cooks and writes, so that they make a pair whose total is more than the parts. And wondering when I was travelling recently in Peru (on which Woodcock wrote twenty years ago) how he does it, I had a few thoughts.

The place is Transylvania or wherever. The Woodcocks arrive by plane or train or car or afoot. They book into their hotel, and Inge calls all the people George wants to meet and talk with. They arrive all at once, and of course it's a little crowded: prime ministers, business execs, peasants and dirt farmers sit on the edge of the bathtub, waiting their turn to talk to George. But there is no confusion. Inge gives them all number cards like

i

at the butcher store. *While this is going on, wives, mistresses and secretaries jam the hotel switchboard. The resulting definitive and much-praised book by George Woodcock is published one week later.*

Of course that is fantasy, which ignores all the hard-slogging footwork armchair readers don't see. But there does seem some quality of magic in the way Woodcock produces books. He is a calm even-tempered person generally; therefore you wouldn't suspect him of being fevered and frenetic inside.

My acquaintance dates from fifteen years ago, when I was encamped in northern B.C. near Woodcock (of all places), with a transistor radio, and heard George Woodcock's verse play Maskerman *on C.B.C. I've forgotten most of that play, except its essential quality, which was a decadent sadness, a quite deliberate over-ripeness, as he has mentioned since. Homer without heroics, if you like. I wrote him an admiring note, as I have to a few other writers I liked. The acquaintance grew into something more than that, and there are times when I think I know him slightly well.*

Woodcock's Selected Poems, *appearing in 1967, were surprising to me. They seemed a strong contrast to his easy-flowing, crystal clear and admirable prose. They bore a strong relation to Auden-MacNeice-Spender-Eliot, etc. My own opinions of English poetry in the 1930's were formed mostly from those people, and I admire them principally for what they said rather than how they said it. It took me a very long time to break away from using conventional metrics myself. After I had done so it took me another long period before I could go back and admire such usage uncritically. I was too stupid then to realize there's an umbilical cord between form and content. Sometime before 1965 I had realized this vital fact.*

Anyway, Woodcock grew up in the English Auden-Spender literary milieu, and wrote in the manner of that slightly earlier day when political philosophy was, perhaps, more literarily important than it is now. Those poets apparently wrote in a form and mood which seemed to debar some areas of the human personality—or so it seemed to me years ago. I now feel that those earlier methods may actually reveal a more fully-rounded persona behind the poems—one not nearly as obvious and blat-

ii

ant as that shown in the work of <u>some addicts of the reality-drug today.</u> ~~my preference~~

Woodcock's *development* is incredibly similar to my own: that is, his early poems are metrical and contained inside the forms he chose for them. But in the last few years he has achieved an ability to go in all prosodic directions, both metric and free forms. You can see that whole development in this book. Whereas I discarded nearly everything I wrote prior to about 1958, because I thought and still think it was junk. I felt I could not say anything of value within rigid forms; whereas Woodcock could. Inside those disciplined early metrics, with understatement being the parallel to present-day throwaway lines, you can find surprising things, every adjective and verb chosen for its absolute employability.

But I won't continue the parallel between George and myself, except to add that we are both similar and dissimilar, his conciseness the opposite of my verbosity. And yet a thousand years of poetry resides in Woodcock much more than it does in me. The implications of his work plunge below the surface of history and philosophy; many times his lightest lines will have anvil-weight. His poems, as he has said elsewhere, have turned around from their earlier forms to become freer; and everything he says now seems inevitably right as to form and content, approaching some more classic definition of what poety ought to be.

And there is such terror in some of these poems!—stemming from what Woodcock calls "a naturally pessimistic side to my mind" which considers "that man may be an evolutionary failure and on his way to join the dinosaurs. . . ." A terror that is prophetic of course. But beside this you must place the onrushing joy he desribes when writing poems, which is caught up in his own life. There is a particular vision of life in some of these pieces. Perhaps it's as well that the excerpted last verse of "Memorandum from Arcadia" doesn't convey the complete vision:

> I shall do the thing the neatest and cleanest way.
> Cord rots soon. I shall drop to the floor.
> I shall be found behind the kitchen door
> Sprawling untidily on the trodden clay.

That is not Auden or Spender or MacNeice, but Woodcock. As is "Poem for Garcia Lorca" which ends: "Remember Lorca, who died only for being Lorca."

After the manner of Auden's "As I Walked Out One Evening" is "Ballad for W.H. Auden" which includes this verse:

> I walked down Granville with Spender
> In a different golden year,
> And Spender said: God and Auden,
> They call each other Dear!

I burst out laughing when I read that passage, because George sorta snuck up on me unexpectedly. But the verse comes from a serious poem, and connects with a later one:

> If your Anglican God has received you
> As Auden or Wystan or Dear
> I know that all is accepted
> With irony, without fear...

It's an evocation and tribute to W.H. Auden, as Auden himself paid his own masterful tribute to Yeats.

I would have liked this short Intro to be my own tribute to George Woodcock, but it is not. That would take someone who understood his complexity better than myself. All I understand is that Woodcock is a great human being, protean and in some understated way, magnificent. He is largely responsible for the regeneration of a country's literature; he is a writer and poet like none presently existing here, nor I suppose, anywhere else. He is also a friend.

Al Purdy

PREFACE

These are poems which, between them, cover a space of more than forty years. The earliest were written round about the beginning of 1935; the most recent was completed in the spring of 1975. Nevertheless, they do not represent a continuity of writing lyrical poetry over the whole of those four decades; for long periods, though I was talkative in other tongues, that special voice was silent. Perhaps three quarters of the poems in this collection were written between 1935 and 1951. Three of them, "Arctic Death", "Reading Tolstoy" and "First Spring on the Island", were written early in the 1960s. The whole of the poems in the last sections, "New Poems", were written between October, 1974 and April, 1975. This does not mean that during the twenty years when I wrote few lyric poems I devoted myself entirely to prose. During the 1960s I wrote three plays in verse, "Maskerman", "The Benefactor" and "The Floor of the Night", a tragedy partially in verse, "Empire of Shadows", and the verse libretto of an opera, "The Bride Ship" for which the music was written by Robert Turner; all these were produced by the Canadian Broadcasting Corporation in its radio programmes, but since I believe dramatic verse needs its context, I have not included in this collection any extracts from them. Doubtless one day the opportunity will come to publish in their entirety those which have not yet appeared in print; "Maskerman" has already been published in *Prism*.

This is a retrospective volume, but not a Collected Poems. It differs largely in its contents from the *Selected Poems* that was published in Canada in 1967. Apart from the section of "New Poems", it contains, mostly in the section entitled "The End Man", poems written in the late 1930s, and lost for many years, so that they first appeared in a group entitled "The Rediscovered Notebook" which was published by *Malahat Review* in 1974. There are also many poems which have not been printed since my last volume before 1967—*Imagine the South*—appeared in Pasadena in 1949. When I assembled my *Selected Poems* in 1967, I adopted a principle of choice which I now realize was too exclusively aesthetic, with the result that many poems inspired by political or moral passion were left out. Some of these, like "The Ruins of London", the elegies for Emma Goldman and Bakunin, the poems about Wales in the Depression and about the experience of being a conscientious objector, I eventually realized represented areas of my life—and I mean my life as a poet—that I could not ignore.

I have arranged the poems in a series of groups which reflect the areas of emotion and experience from which they came, and in each case I have added a prefatory note. The pages that follow now are really intended to explain the kind of double background out of which my work has emerged: the England of the Thirties and Forties, complicated in my case by the presence of Canada, first (as I explain in the opening pages of *Canada and the Canadians*) as a pervasive myth in my boyhood, and later as an experienced reality.

* * *

As far as I can recollect, I wrote my first poem in about 1925, when I was thirteen, moved mainly by the spirit of emulation. I was then living in Marlow, a small town in the Thames Valley; though I was born in Winnipeg, I had divided most of my youth between Marlow and an equally small and even more rustic town in Shropshire, Market Drayton. My people were impoverished peasants—decayed yeomen farmers whose children had found their way into shops and offices (some even—though like Dickens we tried to conceal this—into gentleman's service) and though I went to an ancient grammar school with a tradition of strict caning and of sound training in English literature up to 1830, I was unable—like most young people in my social situation during the 1930s, to attend a university.

Poetry, nevertheless, was in its own way present. Shelley had lived in a house next to my school, where he had entertained Godwin and Peacock and Leigh Hunt, and it was said that under a vast old cedar which shaded both the school quadrangle and the garden of his house he had written *The Revolt of Islam*. Thus poetry was in the air. One became a versifier or a footballer, and I detested football. Periodicals proliferated among us. I became one of the editors of a mimeographed penny journal set up in opposition to the school magazine; the school magazine only published conventional metrical poems, whereas we had heard remotely of free verse and set out to practice it. I have forgotten the title of the magazine, but I can still remember, with intense embarrassment, two lines of one of my own contributions. I remember also the English master, an excellent Miltonist who more than any other person fostered my enthusiasm for literature, looking up from reading it and remarking, sadly and censoriously, "It doesn't even scan"; I rejoiced.

Remember, it was 1925 in small town England. Nobody later than Tennyson was taught in our school, and he was considered the mere shadow of his predecessors; Rupert Brooke was thought a daring modern. *The Waste Land* had been published three years before, but I doubt if anyone in my town had even heard of it. I myself did not encounter it until I was nineteen, six years later. Today, when modern poetry is taught in the schools and is accessible through paperbacks and public readings on a scale unexampled before, I find it hard to believe my own memories of how isolated anyone brought up in an English country town in the 1920s, or even as late as the 1940s, could be from contemporary currents in literature or any other of the arts. I feel that most of the young poets I encounter now start right in at the 1970s, and if they move backward in time that is a later development. I started not later than the 1880s, and by the time I was twenty I had worked my way through an astonishing number of poetic schools. I caught the black romanticism of the Nineties, fled to the country with the Georgians, paid homage to the Dark Gods with D.H. Lawrence, and in the end, as the crowning feat of my career as a youthful pasticheur, composed an imitation *Waste Land*. I still keep the manuscript volumes filled with the hundreds of entirely derivative poems I wrote at that time, and find them invaluable as a kind of literary chronicle in which the inner life, the fantasies and enthusiasms of a lost self are recorded. And surveying my life as a writer, I realize that no period was quite so exciting as that in which I developed, on my own almost entirely, as a kind of time traveller, traversing the decades of other men's experiences, looking at the world every month with different eyes, writing about it every week in a different way, and intoxicated by the inexpressible vividness with which the poetic fancy seemed to endow everything it touched. It was with two impeccably traditional poems that I first achieved publication in the eclectic pages of A.R. Orage's *New English Weekly*. One of them, entitled "Nocturne", began thus:

'Tis even, day's dark requiem,
   The grey gnats dance a rigadoon,
And Venus, like a pendant gem,
   Hangs from the girdle of the moon . . .

In publishing these poems, Orage must have had an idea that I could do something different, for in the desultory correspondence that followed he encouraged me to read Eliot and especially Pound, and through Pound's influence I began to move through the starkness of imagism towards a poetry stripped of archaic affectations, a poetry in which—on however modest a scale—my own observations and experiences spoke directly. It was at this time, round about 1935, that I wrote the earliest of the poems included in this volume—"Summer Fire", "Sawmill", "Winter Wheat". The last two caught the social echoes which by that time it was difficult to avoid even on the long walks over the Buckinghamshire chalkhills that in those days gave me the hints for most of my poems. Appropriately, they were published in a little ephemeral socialist magazine that emanated from High Wycombe.

    I continued to write, still largely in isolation, picking up hints from popular literary magazines like *John O' London's Weekly,* and especially the *Listener,* where Joe Ackerley was beginning to publish Auden and Spender, Edwin Muir and other poets, less remembered, like A.S.J. Tessimond, who fleetingly influenced me. It was in 1938 that I began at last to feel sure that I had found a voice of my own, and in finding it I caught up with my time, for the poems I wrote in that year were accepted by the editors of the leading avant garde magazines, first *New Verse* (with the "Memorandum from Arcadia" which appears in this volume) and then *Twentieth Century Verse* (with "The Island"). At the end of 1938 a London bookseller, Charles Lahr, who had been much involved in avant garde movements since the early 1920s, published my first small collection, *Six Poems*.

I have written already, in *Tamarack Review* and more recently in *Applegarth's Folly*, of the literary circles in which I began to move at that period. Some of the poets I knew, like Spender and Roy Fuller and Dylan Thomas, influenced me in ways that will be evident to anyone who reads this volume, though in the case of Fuller it was largely a question of our moving into the same thematic territory at the same time and exchanging messages. Other poets whom I knew well and liked, such as Herbert Read, Roy Campbell and Kathleen Raine, influenced me hardly at all in poetic terms, though Read, like Orwell, influenced my prose and helped to shape the political persona that began to emerge in my poetry and in my editing during the 1940s.

During the 1930s I had been a concerned and even passionate radical, attached to no party until, in 1938, I joined the Independent Labour Party for a brief period. I distrusted the Communists, who seemed to me either gramophones or inverted snobs, and an admiration for Gandhi which remains with me had led me towards pacifism, which in turn—since it involved putting my personal choice above that of the state —led me into anarchism. In so far as my poetry took on a political tinge during the 1940s, it was pacifism and anarchism that were the evident doctrines. From 1941 onwards, indeed, I became active in the anarchist movement in Britain, and remained so until almost the end of the decade, when I left for Canada.

That departure coincided with a sudden diminution in the urge to write poetry. This happened, at about the same time, to many of the poets who, like me, had begun to appear at the end of the Thirties. Julian Symons, editor of *Twentieth Century Verse* and himself a victim of this loss of power, has suggested that it sprang from our disillusionment at finding the world unchanged after the great war ended. Certainly—as the poems in the first part of this selection will suggest—I saw the future from the vantage point of war-battered London in a somewhat apocalyptic manner, with a new order following on the dramatic destruction of the old, but I believe that in my case there were other reasons for my weakening urge to write poetry than mere political disappointment. First there was the considerable culture shock involved in adjusting to a way of life in western Canada that was unfamiliar and in many ways rather harsh, at least in my special circumstances. And then there was the fact that on the very day of my arrival in Canada a person who had embodied almost everything I stood for during the 1940s died in brilliant and beautiful youth. I found that I could not find a poetic expression for my feelings, and that failure kept me silent as a poet for a decade and decisively turned me towards prose.

As I have said, I began to write verse again in the early 1960s, but shortly afterwards I became interested in drama, and that consumed for a number of years any urge towards poetry that I found stirring within me. The dramas, to a great extent, carried on the vein of social criticism that appeared in much of the early poetry and in the verse of the intervening period.

I have now begun to write lyric poems again, and it is perhaps not without significance that, just as a deep emotional shock cut off the flow of inspiration in 1949, or rather diverted it into prose, so a less dramatic but equally moving set of personal circumstances, which I have no intention of describing, has set me writing poetry once more.

I.

ANARCHIST ELEGIES

The apocalyptic vision was an essential element in my poetry, and in that of many others, during World War II and the years immediately preceding it. The Luftwaffe raids on London seemed to provide the model for a destruction of the old society, and my mood—expressed in poems like "Waterloo Bridge" and "The Ruins of London"—was one of mingled sorrow that a city I loved should be falling down and burning, and of anticipation—expressed in "Sand" and "Sunday on Hampstead Heath"—of the new world that might come into being. "Waterloo Bridge" led me into a consideration, however rudimentary, of the personal attitudes that might take one through such a passage of social transformation, but the poem also had its closely personal elements, for it was related to my mother's sudden and lonely death in the early months of the war and to the death of Trotsky, which shocked me even though I was far from being his partisan. Other images of destruction and transformation of course take their place in this section; the poems on the depressed areas of South Wales, written in 1938-9, show that the sense of the self-destruction latent in our society was with me even then, and "Tree Felling" carries the image into the relations between man and nature. It was appropriate, given such an apocalyptic inclination, that I should dedicate poems to such apostles of regeneration through the destruction of an old, unjust society as Michael Bakunin and Emma Goldman, at the same time as I set out to record the inner feelings of the pacifist who mourned the necessity by which "The kind and the killer shall share one fate."

I should add that I turned to poems of this kind quite independently of the group, led by Henry Treece, who called themselves New Apocalyptics, though we had enough in common for me to contribute to their magazines.

SAND

In this air serene
Serfs who built the towers
Shall not live again
Or ghosts speak in the wires.

Yellow sand has drowned
Towers, parks and streets,
Flowered, fecund ground,
Rocks with ammonites.

And from tawny soil
Geometric pines
Siphon turgid sap
Through ascetic veins.

But stark pines shall share
Fate of walls and spires
When the eroding wind
Sweeps these sandy shores.

And heroes who survive
The obsolescent wars
Shall rebuild the white
Streets and symbolic towers.

SUNDAY ON HAMPSTEAD HEATH

Underfoot on the hill the water spurts
Thickly out of the brilliant matted grasses
Where the slopes fold in groins and thighs of earth
And the winter sunlight in thin golden masses
Falls through the lunging wind that swings the skirts
Of the girls walking with their soldiers over the Heath.

A group of dwarf fir trees marks the crest
With boughs like drowner's hands that claw the sky.
Far down the slope a white springboard rears
Its gaunt and skeleton frame above the grey
Tossed pool where in summer the boys raced
But where now only the ducks bob, resting their oars.

Leaning their weight on London, the smoky roofs
Below the hill stretch out their infinite folds,
A stony sea, far in miasmic depth
Where men sleep out their empty dreams of deeds,
And towers and domes, surging like green reefs,
Rise up heroic and powerful in their sloth.

Here on the hilltop my friends and I sit down.
They talk of prisons; the conversation falls
And I saw: "One evening we must drink at the Spaniards."
I do not know what they are thinking as their heels
Kick out the turf and their gaze creeps over the scene,
Peering through the smoke for the customary landmarks.

But, going away in my mind from their shut faces,
Away from the quiet hilltop and the leisurely men
Digging in their new gardens below in the little valley,
I enter the forest of rooftops; under the grimy stone
I walk among the pipedreams of men in braces
Reading in Sunday newspapers the end of faith and folly.

And in the broken slums see the benign lay down
Their empty useless loves, and the stunted creep
Ungainly and ugly, towards a world more great
Than the moneyed hopes of masters can ever shape.
In the dead, grey streets I hear the women complain
And their voices are sparks to burn the myth of the state.

And here where my friends talk, and the green leaves spurt
Quietly from waterlogged earth, and the dry leaves bud,
I see a world may rise as golden as Blake
Knew in his winged dreams, and the leaves of good
Burst out on branches dead from winter's hurt.
Then the lame may rise and the silent voices speak.

good image conveys political vision.

many of the poems of a piece with other social & political writings - limits accessibility?

TREE FELLING

The bright axe breaks the silence in the wood.
The ivory chips spray over crushed nettles,
And the red slender pine sways and totters
Shuddering its boughs in the chill of death.

All down the hill the yellow teeth of stumps
Stud the tramped moss and broken willow herb;
The piled long boles point northward to the Pole,
Their fragrant lymph seeping from broken veins.

And borne away in the blue wake of tractors,
The lopped trees leave for ever their fitting landscape;
Soon they will grow again in the underground valleys
Where the naked miners crawl under a sagging sky.

And here the ploughs will traverse, as in Carthage
Marking the end of a kingdom, the day of the squirrel
And the blue jay chattering along the mossed alleys
Between the still pines. The silence of felted needles,

Spawning in ugly toadstools and sick brown orchids,
Has ended that seemed unending. Cyclic transition
Will reign on the hillside, with bare and ice-baked winter
And multitudinous summers under the whispering corn.

WATERLOO BRIDGE

The arms flicker like signals in the sun,
The rhythmic oars flash silver up the stream,
And through the green and stormy lakes of plane
Glide the black angels and the ghosts of peace.
On Waterloo Bridge I am thinking of a name
Written in lead, I am thinking of ashes,
I am thinking of graveyards billowed like a lake,
I am thinking of death's searchlights that will flower the dark.

And, again, I am thinking of the angels and William Blake.
I imagine Blake in his chariot over St. Paul's,
And Swinburne fast as a plane above the Park,
Homing from spurious sin to smugness at The Pines.
Donne in his shroud is descending on Sadler's Wells
And through this peopled air pulse spectral tunes,
The infant Mozart and decrepit Handel
Competing in the wind's orgasmic rise and fall.

These spectres say our errors are returning,
Snake-eyed, to bury us. They say only our hells
Are repetitive, and in vain we long
For the rebirth of momentary heavens.
In the symbolic silence of the bells
As the hour strikes, softly they lean and warn
Against our hopes, our loves, our petty goods.
Then float to higher heavens, balloons and gods.

This is the preposterous hour when Caesars rise,
Bleeding, from their beds in the burning sea.
The dead are cashing in on all our follies.
They are not men and women, they are not divine,
These spirits bred of our own villainy.
It is ourselves who gibber at the pane,
Clanking across our age magnetic fetters,
Skywriting madness in incandescent letters.

6

This evening aviators crumple on killing earth,
This evening Trotsky is dying. Blood for blood
Seeping from birth and cataclysmic death
Mars the pale sky where gulls and flags are flying,
And love is failing where but hate is good.
This evening, I perceive, we are all dying,
We are all dying, like Wilde, beyond our means,
Dying, as sheep, for our folly rather than sins.

A malady like a journey is killing us slowly.
On the long inconstant travels of the mind
Towards the paradise we are approaching daily
But never reach, on endless days in the sun
Walking the deserts of our insular land
Between the pectoral hills and the salt lagoon,
We are haunted each evening by time's gorgon face
The sickness of change is rotting our lives like ice.

I make the image of death, symbolical god
With spear and book, the angel of every aspect,
The joking fisher, devil with vulpine head
And mutable image of deity and man.
I imagine also the impersonal fact
Knitting the end of a maturing plan
And insubstantial force whose iron need
Draws down to earth the flower sapped with seed.

I imagine the frozen gesture of the loved
Made in the silent room, the rigid hand
Rising to the crying mouth and bowed head
Solid and grey as stone. The fearful lives of the lonely
Fail in an emptiness that is an end
More for the left. To those who have lived only
In their own hearts death must always be near
Among evil quiet and the steady voices of fear.

I see the plane caught in crossed hands of light,
Lurched in white spits of fire, till sudden flame
Splits in the sky, an instant hell of fate
Tearing the flesh and metal, mind and life
Into atomic agony and dusty doom.
I see the grasping hand above the wave,
The face in the fiery window, the ragged cross
Of the climber spread beneath the precipice.

grotesque, violent images frequently the best

But these are not the death in all the faces.
Not the stiff slain, but we the living die
Daily among the city's beautiful houses
And mortal streets, under the knowing speech
Of clocks and the togaed gestures of the high ?
Snatching with metal hands a world beyond our reach.
Time is our death. Our death is also life.
We are slain by what it is a death to leave.

For us, my love, there is no peculiar escape.
The pass is kept and frontiers of the mind
Barred by the unseen we cannot overleap.
I on this bridge, you in the speeding train
Framed in the window in your farewell stand,
Travel the one evil journey of the brain
For the perennial peak. As others striving
We share in their insidious death of living.

For us the sound of history is growing faint,
For us the distances are opening and now is as soon
Past as it is beginning. On this tremulous point
Crowded like angels in the schoolman's mind
We hang in sufferance of the hastening sun,
We hang in sufferance of the sweeping hand.
There are no far lands for us, as we await,
Already dead, death to confirm our fate.

This is an autumn whose leaves are falling iron
Shed by a deciduous sky upon our hope.
The metal leaves are blotting out the sun,
The falling sky is crushing out all love
In this sad land wherein our futures weep.
In this dry land our weeping cannot save
Only the stone heart is immune from pain,
Only the automaton outlives the steel rain.

So we are dead who could not make in life
That peace in beauty which our gods ordained,
So we are dead beneath the withered leaf
Of worlds aborted by our winter's stroke,
Our thin delusions by now's evening stained.
Cursed by a present that in weakness broke
In blood and dust, we also were too weak
To shun the common nemesis of the sick.

Yet I recall the evenings marked in time,
The whispered intimations and the vague fingers
Of youth, when landscapes, as my thoughts, were calm
And when the dusky mirages of heaven
Cloaked in their mist the bloody teeth of dangers,
And the evil eye that orders odd or even.
Time was the voices speaking from the wood,
Fiery chariots rising through the splitting cloud.

And from the bridge, above the windy planes,
The flickering signals and the grey river,
Above the girls, above the silvery vanes
Pointing the winds set for homeric wests,
Above now, above this pointed here,
I see the statued rising from their rests,
The famous rising again above the city
That dies beneath their iron galaxy.

[handwritten: evidence of the decadent sensibility]

9

[handwritten: many images, feelings remain indistinct, not vivid or gripping]

These are the praised, remembered in verse and stone,
Multiplied in the actions of the living,
These are the great whose earthly death has grown
In an existence greater than their death.
Above the striving and above the raving
They soar, as vast as gods, as light as breath.
I know they did not fail, they did not die
As we who live our dying blasphemy.

I know no world infected their desires
Or sapped their deeds. Lapped into their own souls,
Strong within strong, coiling their moving fires
In metal might, in spiritual rock,
From the involvulate power of their wills
They sprang above the flesh, the chance and luck
Of daily evils undermining love,
And the deepening lesser deaths we live.

So they defeat the double death of man,
Our present death and death that makes an end
Of blood and monument. The lantern brain
Lit them a way I see that we must run
If we, my love, would live beyond the hand
That coils our life into a twist of pain.
Our selves within our hearts we must create
Like seeds in flowers and flowers involvulate.

We who are dying, like phoenix on the flame
Must burn our now and re-enact each self
Out of the agony of expiring same.
We must erect, within the circled soul
A centre warm to our peculiar life,
Signed by our individual breath and will.
We, as the rose, must blossom at the heart,
Closed like the flesh sea flower against death's hurt.

Then, as the growing music of the deaf
Erects its heaven within the closing skull,
May we achieve the harmonies that live
Beyond our little death, re-edify
The subtle architecture of the will,
Live above life, who die and daily die;
In the blank chaos of the faltering hour
Make of our blood the Babylonian tower.

Inside Vienna, as the cannon spat
Mortal destruction on the breaking walls,
Death on the child's brick halls, Beethoven sat
With ears unhearing but within the mind
Music unbroken heard. The interlacing hells
In and without the city were unkind,
But in the room, the chamber of his brain,
Music outgrew the immanance of pain.

Here is the map and symbol of our way.
Not a man lives who has not, under fire
Of steel or love, felt the desire to die
As we who die, the millions sham alive.
But music in the spiritual ear
Ignores the deadly world and thus, my love,
Breathing, as gods, our mountain air of truth,
We may escape the daily hour of death.

On Waterloo Bridge I am thinking of a name
Written in fire. Yet fires end in ash
And here I wonder if our hopes are dream,
If voices whispering in the evening river
Speak in my ear the prophecies I wish,
If still for us death is the only saviour
From the mean lesser deaths our failures make
Under the deadly flowering of the dark.

THE RUINS OF LONDON

Those hurrying taxis, lovers fingering thighs
Towards the termini of journeys and desires,
Pass with fixed stares of round, inanimate eyes,
Irrelevant this evening as the dying saurian;
And old men homing, senile and unfair,
Tramp the cold avenues of cruel stone.
Only the unformed young and the formless old
Wear now the fabulous stones of gainless gold.

In the mock arson of the falling sun
The girls, lovely and ugly, tap their heels
Escaping in subways from the stinging rain
And the hour's fear of the returning bomber.
For these, the youths, the dotards and the girls,
Dinners are waiting and the cinema
Prepares a drug—more sinister than god—
To render hearts as docile as the dead.

For this is the city where death had domination,
Whose mansions were the grandiose tombs of youth,
Grey catacombs where freedoms slept in line,
Poisoned with gold or strangled by the law,
Granite sarcophagi of love and truth
Where the divine lay slain and stuffed with straw.
Death wore disguise before. We did not miss
Our unlived lives or feel his quiet kiss.

City most lovely in twilight or the dawn,
Where the blind grope like toads and the mad
Limp like devils, where the poor and fearful spawn
Under the earth, anticipating graves,
City, when your red evening on my head
Falls like a breath, like desiccated leaves,
How shall I view the wounds upon your walls,
Your bloody minarets and disembowelled halls?

Ignoring the lecherous idylls of the old
And colourful predilections of the rich and time,
I walk the dusty pavements drenched with blood
And scarred with flame twice in a city's life.
I see the archways built on sweat and crime
Breaking over the knees of Europe's strife
And Wren's white splintered pediments remain
Above the altars prayers could not sustain.

The public hands of frozen clocks declare
Perpetual and apocalyptic instants
Of crashing walls and towers flung through air.
The supple planes that bent before the blast
Are green above the fallen monuments,
The metal gods of privilege and caste
Whose eloquent tongues could not foretell the ends
Death's cunning wrought through their own fleshless hands.

The glassless windows hang like birds in trees.
The avalanches of stone balance as boxers
For the careless tread under the hanging eaves.
The rusty girders twist themselves like worms
Above that dry debris of safes and ledgers
Spread under dust in gold's deserted rooms
Where the typist's mirror hangs upon its nail
Reflecting boughs that bud where towers fall.

Lovely at last in sorrow the city stands
Niobe over her dead. What memories burn
Through time towards this hour, towards these ends
Where words become Phoenix, where our deeds congeal
In rock like ancient footprints, cannot turn
The dying pitiful past upon its heel.
The wounds of change transmute both man and race
As iron erodes the city's stony face.

Shall we open our veins and die like Romans
Sinking under despair in sleepy crimson baths?
Shall we project our journeys to new lands,
Seeking our hope beyond the far and future?
Shall we sit in towers and ponder abstract truths
While men bat-shouldered, cloaked and sinister
Prepare their childish and irrelevant schemes
To kill the priests and poison all the streams?

Death's tocsin rings the blood! What bodies fall
Under this rubble cannot rise to love!
Though we may build our future towers tall
To tip the sky like Babel, time will grant
No respite in decaying, age will leave
No man immune from the attentive ant.
Caught in death's gambit all our struggles end;
Cities and men checked by the same sure hand.

THE ANNOUNCER'S SPEECH

Forget the flowers like faces, seeds like skulls,
   The leaves like bayonets and bulbs like bombs,
Forget the ingenious noses hiding holes,
   The sharks' teeth fringing desiccated gums,
Forget devil and god, for this happy day
They walked out of town and went to stay.

You'll have happiness now, when no Groucho faces
   Tempt you to good or frighten to evil,
When no more orders from demons or angels
   Detail to die or, worse than dying, kill.
God skulks in Heaven, devil in Hell,
The rules are flyblown. No-one hears the bell.

You can grow roses now—there'll be no more blight.
   You can carry out plans for the lily pond.
You can write the interrupted five-act play.
   You can cease taking pills to make the heart strong.
You need never run again for the eight o'clock train
Now the Golden Age has fallen like backstage rain.

You are washed in the blood and clothed in the light,
   You are led by the lamb to the fields of joy,
Where you'll never meet want or work again,
   Bombs in the air or mines in the bay.
Death followed devil and god, this happy day
When they walked out of town and went to stay.

WARTIME EVENING IN CAMBRIDGE

Silhouette of elms against an eggshell evening.
The green Cam slithers beneath me, the yellow girl
Rubs my shoulder, and the uniforms in blue
Direct their dummies to the ultimate kill.

Worn corners of cloisters, walls and turrets
Supporting space. The inexplicable voids of age.
But heavy feet are fettered; under the gateways
Shadows shining like iron maintain their siege.

Skies snow black rooks upon the leafless trees.
The jackdaws rustle to sleep on studious houses.
Mass-souled, the starlings throb towards the fen,
To the night that brings more deadly wings than theirs.

What Marxian spectre lays its beard on the evening?
What twilight have we committed? What blank sin
Broken upon the earth to rage for pardon?
What blood drips what inexpiable stain?

The boys that are marked to die, and the mad women
Driving their lovers to death for a cheap song,
And the men who will be leaded names on gravestones;
Passing, these cannot solve the brooding evening's wrong.

And watching the fading colours, the dimmed horizon,
The white faces becoming vague under the shadow,
I see an age that will not end for many
Draw its own death like a blind across a window.

POEM FOR MICHAEL BAKUNIN

The wayfaring tree walks heavy for the winter,
The multifaceted eyes of evenings
Lean down into their darkness
Like lights on sinking ships
And the whistling ghosts follow us in the streets.

The black and white of gravestones under the lash
Of flowing branches hurling bobs of life
Seeds in the mind the morrows feared and far
That soon shall join their tips
Into a day more burning than the sun.

For that dry future, when these tiny flames
Grow into one to burn both fear and hope
And when life's day spills on a ruined land
The iron growth of stars where green guns grew,
Shall be more violent than our eyes can hold.

And in that instant, when time's two worlds meet
And day's destructive urge breaks down the dark
To set a furnace in a dying age,
Our little selfish loves and days shall wane
Beneath a glowing and perpetual noon.

ELEGY FOR EMMA GOLDMAN

For those who, magnolia tall, confront us,
Stately and pale, gods of a golden earth,
And south's inheritors of suns and status,
There is no place among the quiet shadows
Of grey men drenched in brine and crowned with dirt,
There is no kingdom in the drowning furrows,
Or under the brimming towers, ambiguous trees
Where the dead water and women find their peace.

Sad are cities where freedom stings like cancer;
Not for the fortunate their eyeless evenings
Where tears are stagnant and death stands as a fencer
With the ready point of doom above the helpless.
Here those in silver gendered and sired by kings
Are blind to the dark stigmata on rotting faces,
And their happy superior days end without meaning
In iron forests where only the drunken sing.

The trees starting in semaphores from my earth
Signal a life more simple and more wise
Than those who were happy, without thought, from birth.
So you, Black Emma, walking the evil streets
With horror etched as a map upon your eyes
And the blood of anger rising in trees from your breasts
Carried a need as single in your heart
As the sap rising in the Spring's young heat.

Kinetic as a plant the purpose rose
High from your head among the sterile stones
Of many million people and no hopes.
Not for the feckless were the flowers you bore,
Not for the dying waiting for dead men's bones,
Not for the visages consumed by fear.
Only for the evil cities and the grey, trodden men,
For the poets and drowning women your black blooms shone.

An age bursting like a well at winter's depth
Spills on the cities its sad and brutal night.
The day we are born to is ebbing from the earth,
The day that gave our comfort and their need
And the common living death in the hard sunlight
Where beauty wilted in the noon of greed.
The evening ends. We cannot see what day
Lies past the night we enter under an evil sky.

But in that day those tongues we shall remember
That spoke, in the dead years, of pride and freedom;
We shall remember their goodness and their anger.
Our minds will hear them from the quiet grave;
Their dreams will shape the margins of our futures
Till mental cords shall drop from every slave.
Then you will walk the daylight of our thought.
Now our deeds remember you in the night.

PACIFISTS

The icy, empty dawn cracks in the fields
Under our labouring feet. We cross the fallow
With billhooks on our shoulders sloped like guns,
Drawing dark lines in rime white as we go.

Standing in filthy ditches in leaking boots,
We fell the towering hedges like Jericho walls
Under the blast of day. Around our feet
The water seeps and numbs through invisible holes.

Strange we have come, from library and office.
Hands that had never toiled, myopic eyes
And sloping backs revolt in an alien time.
Under a dead sky we expiate our oddness.

Having left friends and substitutes for love
In the leaning fragments of a distant city
We tread the furrows of infertile fields
And rediscover our pasts in a wet country.

Under our ineffectual misery, our boredom
And the empty sequence of unprivate days,
The lost squalors of the city become our end.
The cause that brought us dwindles. We hate blank skies,

Biting wind and the black bones of trees,
The promise of spring as a green omen of toil.
We rest our billhooks and talk of a starlit town
As the weak sun breaks on the land without a hill.

THE CONCHY'S LAMENT

Rain slashes the brown clods of my acre,
Breaking tilth for the seed and avid roots.
I sit in the gloomy doorway of my shed,
Lighting my pipe and taking off my boots,

And think of yesterday's blue and the shouting planes
Courting like kestrel over my digging back,
Dancing to death down the roaring air,
Screaming through cirrus above eye's peak.

So in this gloom my heart a seed of sorrow
Grows towards graves and through the gaping skull.
My hands can feed the plant and feed the children;
They cannot sustain the dead against death's will.

Through veils of rain the stranger at the gate
Waits invisibly, but will not be late,
While the wet wind wails its descant of hate:
"The kind and the killer shall share one fate."

LANDORE

Fume-bitten no grassness of mountains,
barrenness not of summer,
meant the reek of copper rising up the valley,
seeping into houses, drying child lungs,
eating the cheek of beauty
but keeping factories prosperous, bringing
dividends to shareholders, to the workers
bread in belly, freedom from absolute want, a little pleasure.

Now the down of grass sprouts, fire galvanic
bursts the yellow flowers, harsh green
new moss veins the stone brows,
birds nest on the mountain,
the air is pure and hunger is in the valley,
dereliction
of sag-roof factory and smokeless stack,
children suffering now the flaccid unfed belly,
young men squatting for talk in the lee of walls,
the slow round of mountain and stone-grey street,
pitch-and-toss in the slag heap,
walks by the scummed river,
The Red Flag sung like a dirge,
and the public library now and again of a morning.

THE SILENT MILLS OF PENTRE

Behold the angina pectoris of an age!
The thousand metal replicas of the time's heart
slow already in bodies of brick and earth
until as pistons is the land's pulse still.

Thus is the start. Man's creatures dying first
crystal his end, and general stasis spreads
slowly, by town and land, by man and man.
Man dies.   Only the men survive
to feel the insidious smothering of time
shut the world into an airless trap,
to fear the pangs that split their private breasts
presage the evening when the willing fuse
bursts the heart of the old from Pentre to Rome.

STEEL VALLEY, 1938

War husks its rumours, and the yellow scurf
Of gorse scabs mountains over men who smote
Steel and trod surer feet on slag than turf.

But in their valley, where the fume clouds float
Only in memory and past-praising speech,
These men have learnt life to a meagre rote,

Achieve negation, but no wider reach
Span towards anger. Theirs the needy urge
That prompts the searching of the hungry leech

And tilts the sunning cups of dingy spurge,
Theirs the blunt memory of singeing blast
And prosperous creeping of the slag tip's verge.

Essentials only, cold and hunger, last.
Here stand no idols for the inconoclast.

CHRISTMAS SONNET, 1939

From this sad planet, where the tragic are
Set in their tears like silence, I regard
Black space and every far and frigid star,
Whose brightest fire in distance shines like cold,
And know in envy white's celestial spray
That spreads as drops each bloodless, manless world.

Once stars as angels sang to this dark day,
When planets signed the quick essential man,
But blood and clay submerge the high and free
And no worlds sign or sing, but burn again
Millenial fire or cool to styptic ash
Unbitten by the dirty tread of men.
What gaseous gods there live, what fleshness flesh,
Earth's lord is lovely only in his wish.

THE LITTLE TREES

The little trees, steepening up the hill,
With empty basins spread beneath their boughs,
Show the contour of the vanished wall.

Each spring the dwindling veterans planted rose
And paper cornflowers by the upgrown road.
Now, only the agaric grows.

For the veterans are dead or old
In the valley where the young once more
Toil day and night,
With iron, blood and gold
To build again the falling wall of fear.

II.

MYTHS

In the late Thirties in England we were much given to the writing of myth poems. The work of my friends and contemporaries, like Roy Fuller and Julian Symons and Ruthven Todd, contains many examples of them. But there was, I think, an essential difference between our myth-poetry and what has been called mythopoeic poetry among Canadian writers in recent decades. We knew our Frazer, of course, and by about 1941 I had begun, under Herbert Read's influence, to read Jung with attention, so that I was well aware of the resonances that myths aroused, both in terms of the human past and in terms of one's own inner consciousness. In writing a myth poem one was laying at least an ironic claim to universal understanding. But even more, I think, we regarded myths as models in which we could use existing components cavalierly, in new combinations, to create pictures of human situations, of psychological states. The familiarity of symbols and of legends turn them into a kind of shorthand by which it became possible to convey a great deal more, in a concise, oblique manner, than could have been done in a more discursive form. Sometimes I would use a known classical myth, sometimes a dramatic historic incident, like the defeat of Hannibal or the death of Lassalle, sometimes a scene from a painting, and sometimes an invented situation that aroused a visual image with appropriate universal associations, as in "The Hero", "The Agitator" and "The Fugitive". The myth attracted me also, I think, because it allowed a controlled use of the exotic: a disciplined Gothicism.

THE ISLAND

The oars fell from our hands. We climbed the dark
   Slopes of kelp to the stairway up the rock.
Scott went first, grasping the fraying rope.
   The rest of us followed, dragging the iron rack.

The crest was bare, but after a scanty search
   In a bird's burrow we found the hunted man.
His flesh was naked and hard as barren earth,
   His arms like scythes. His eyes spoke like a gun.

Before him we retired, unmanned by fear.
   Unarmed, he seemed to move with harmful light.
Scott only stood, shaming us in the end.
   The fugitive surrendered without fight.

We laid him on the painful rack, stretched tight
   His limbs and bound his feet and wrists with wire,
Set leaden weights upon his sunken chest
   And tied his head down by the matted hair.

We turned the cranks and wrenched him hour by hour.
   In silence he endured. He would not speak
Of the hidden ore. At last his joints burst out
   And jetting from the ruptures fire broke.

Then lay before us on the rigid rack
   Straw limbs and a horse's polished skull.
Gulls mocked as walked away across the sea
   The man we hunted but could not keep or kill.

We threw the rack into the hungry surf
   And hacked the turf in anger with our swords.
Then re-embarking on our fruitless voyage,
   We left the island to the mice and birds.

IMAGINE THE SOUTH

Imagine the South from which these migrants fled,
Dark-eyed, pursued by arrows, crowned with blood.
Imagine the stiff stone houses and the ships
Blessed with wine and salt, the quivering tips
Of spears and edges signalling in the sun
From swords unscabbarded and sunk in brine,
Imagine the cyclamen faces and yielding breasts
Hungered after in a dead desert of icy mists,
Imagine, for though oblivious, you too are cast
Exile upon a strange and angry coast.

Going into exile away from youth,
You too are losing a country in the south,
Losing, in the red daylight of a new shore
Where you are hemmed by solitude and fear,
The loving faces far over a sea of time,
The solid comfort and the humane dream
Of a peaceful sky, the consoling patronage
And the golden ladder to an easy age;
All these are lost, for you too have gone away
From your Southern home upon a bitter journey.

There is no home for you marked on the compass.
I see no Penelope at the end of your Odysseys,
And all the magic islands will let you down.
Do not touch the peaches and do not drink the wine,
For the Dead Sea spell will follow all you do,
And do not talk of tomorrow, for to you
There will only be yesterday, only the fading land,
The boats on the shore and tamarisks in the sand
Where the beautiful faces wait, and the faithful friends.
They will people your mind. You will never touch their hands.

ARCTIC DEATH

High in the grey, and golden gyrating,
Osprey and eagle wheeled above those
Blond explorers whom northern autumn
Closed in and caught too late for leaving.

Hare's fur blanched, marsh slime set granite,
Bushes burnt crimson, charred grey for winter;
All game had gone, by stealth retreating
To tree lines provident with lichen.

Too long they'd waited along the traplines.

So in bleak barren, tempest-bitten,
Bivouacs built, a wealth of corpses—
Fox and marten in wall-width morticed,
Matted fine furs in aspic winter.

There chewed raw fish, shrugged cold, despaired,
Yawned in the daze of snow, and slept;
Like silver kings in that locked north
Waited the sweet, corrupting spring.

BREUGHEL

Snow falls in ash across a smoky sky.
The dun-clad hunters, crossing a white valley,
Follow the compass noses of their hounds
To the bare copse on the little pointed hills.

The crisp air colours their lined, cunning faces,
Intent on the end of the hunt and the genial evening
Swilling on the dirty straw of a welcome hovel.
Thus they will consume the slow years to senility.

Thus they will cross the narrow valleys of days,
Following the quarry perennial and elusive,
Until one evening they enter a closed valley
And, finding no outlet and the entrance drift-bound,

Sink into the snow sleep of death.
Looking upon their moment set in paint,
Held up from death by hands long laid away,
I see our future mirrored in their past,

The long and fruitless days on cold landscapes,
The quiet hills, deceptive valleys of love,
And the unnamed quarry eluding every chase,
Until the last hunt clogs our eyes with snow.

THE HERO

Out of the east the hero came,
tall as a tree and swift as a flame,
lithe as water and lovely as cream.

But his eyes were fire and his tongue was steel,
his finger a flag and his voice a bell
and magic to rats and men his will.

He slew the kings and the titled drones,
felled the chapels and gods of stone
and made his roads with the sacred bones.

He used his guns to bring down rain,
fed the poor with the royal grain,
killed the church and the dread of thirteen.

But he died, and they buried his bones in gold,
His laws were frozen in a changeless code
and his name was God on the lips of the old.

Till another hero came from the east
and threw his bones for the dogs to feast.

THE AGITATOR

The yellow flowers broken by his feet
Sent up their acrid warning to his heart;
The wordless signpost like a rotting tongue
Gave him no answer, and he had no chart

Written upon his mind, behind the eyes.
The thickets where the clear-voiced blackcap sang,
The little sedge-rimmed pools between the trees
Led him to a new country where his foes were strong.

Somewhere at the end there lay a city
Where the women would greet him in their smoky houses,
Holding the knife hidden within the girdle
Or offering slow venom in coloured beautiful glasses.

And in that city he must reject their cunning,
Outwit the foxy men who watched his step
And carry his doctrine quietly in his heart
Until the hour when daily thought would stop,

Crowds would see visions, and his thoughts, like birds
Burdened with messages, would find their homes.
Already in mind he saw the breasts of men
Opening to free the phoenix of their dreams.

The little hills that lay along his path
Shed their long shadows as the evening fell.
Beyond their wall, west by the setting sun,
The paper gunmen waited for their kill.

THE FUGITIVE.

The stranger leant on his door, and through his window
The enemy eyes of stars burnt into his sleep.
Surrounded by foes, plucking his fear about him,
He dreamed desperately of a friendly future.

He saw the quiet bodies and empty eyes
That carried no treason.   He saw enormous forests
Where races could vanish, and the far lovely islands
Divided by turbulent seas from the fearful mainland.

He saw the ice pyramid where the naked Yogin
Entered a solitary and impersonal heaven.
He saw the gardens hanging on ultimate cliffs
And the lovers alone and together over a distant sea.

But over all the journeys of his dreams
The hostile stars looked with their million eyes,
And his travels ended in that sleepless city
Where all men watched him, all women were false and bland.

THE RETURN OF ODYSSEUS

Poor was the village and wet the way
When X came back last Easter Day.

Scant was the food and thin the beer
When X came back with his comrade Fear.

Strange were the kids and the old men daft
When X returned like an empty craft.

The women went white and screamed of a ghost
When X came limping in from the coast.

And the wrestlers shuddered in church and house
When X returned to his home and spouse.

The clock was striking, the hour was fate,
When X came in at the garden gate.

Time was failing, the end was sure
When X was knocking the kitchen door.

The spouse went mad, the other went dumb,
When X stood there from kingdom come.

For the house was full and full the bed
When X returned from the far and the dead.

But he was lame and he was blind,
X moaning there in the bitter wind,

And unseen the face, unknown the way,
When X came back that Easter Day.

So they gave him pence and gave him food
And set his face on the inland road,

And time restarted, the men went sane,
When X walked on in the wind and rain.

GODS

That was the plain, where grass instead of hair
   Grew on the heads of gods, whose temples stood
Phallic and gleaming in the vast morass,
   Held from its hunger by great rafts of wood.

At night the gods went in their iron trucks
   Along the causeways, paved with frozen flesh
And built on cubes of papier-maché rock,
   Into the villages beyond the marsh.

There they were offered nails and human teeth,
   Foreskins and crutches of the grateful lame.
Virginities were broken on their knees.
   The village feuds were started in their name.

But through all this the gods impassive sat.
   The wheels that bowed their heads and moved their jaws,
Had long been rusty and their limbs were set
   Hard as their own outdated changeless laws.

METAURUS

Proud with his pachyderms filing the perilous passes
brought Barca Romeward fear and bleak danger
dire of arson and fire mouths feeding on riches,
corrosion of famine, ravishment of the nubile, terror
of arrows at noon, swords in the dark, blood
on the oak leaves, on the reeds of Arno,
terror of trodden flowers, of dust to strange feet stirring
out of Capua, of eagles broken, emblems annihilated.

Fire in the veins, a furnace in the reins,
burning a pyre of pride across the brain,
Trebia to Trasimene triumph ran like fire!
Cannae's fulfilment! In an enemy land
Victory! Victory in the garden of Rome!

But weak eyes after, in hostile hills
marches to terror of ambush, watches
on bare peninsulas, sleepless camps,
signals from cliffs, the mirages of rumour,
over the palisades the head hurled, agony
of recognition by firelight, message of Metaurus
said by dry lips, visions in carrion eyes
of goalless marches, nightfalls of defeat,
starved tongues, the flight from oasis to desert,
the chase narrowing, the dead whispering,
the lipped cup opening immortality.

FERDINAND LASSALLE

His past was always with him. In his blood
He carried the messenger with the poisoned knife
Ready to gash his brain and drain his heart.
The speaking statue attended all his triumphs.

Down the soft Rhineland roads and through the shouts
Of little German towns he rode with garlands,
The leader of an age, the good disciple
Who stole his teacher's credit for his own.

He was audacious and a people loved him.
His lameness was the perpetual memento.
His triumph ran through the heart of Germany.
Death's triumph ran through his rotting heart.

The messenger led him, one summer morning,
To the empty field on the edge of the city
Where time was waiting with words of lead.
He died and Marx rejoiced at his dying.

FOR AN ELDER STATESMAN

Fishing beside the ends of choked canals,
 He did not know Troy fallen, Lenin dead;
Only the swing of seasons did he feel,
 Petals to leaves to snowflakes on his head.

And, after death, subaqueous heavens him held
 And dank havens of his earthly wish,
Sunk in the glory of eternal gloom,
 One with Christ, the elemental fish.

III.

MEMENTOS

Much of the work of most poets is involved in the exploration of memories or incidents of personal importance. Sometimes, in my case, the remembered image remained dominant, as in "Summer Fire" and "Roses and Christmas Roses", but those were early poems, and later the urge to manipulate the memory or the impression so as to give it more aesthetic interest, or to make it a more adequate paradigm, or to draw some philosophic point, grew dominant. What began, in "Ancestral Tablet", as a recollection of one of my grandfathers came in the end to incorporate features of both my grandfathers, and so turned into an epitaph on a rural generation. "Snow in London" became an image for the shame of human relationships, as "First Spring on the Island" became an image for the shame of man's relationship with other living beings. Reading a sentance in *Anna Karenina*, by a Proustian development, produced a poem about remembered childhood, and so, each in its way, the other poems led through the narrow gates of their original impulses into special gardens or caverns of the mind.

ANCESTRAL TABLET

Night when mares escaping fought in the lane
Where apples went to fields in the glut year,
We talked in the sandstone kitchen as glabrous dawn

Woke birds and the house. Crops and the threatened war,
The evil milk laws, then his distant youth,
Building the line, and the Homeric poacher.

He was the boy who wrestled rural Goliath,
The tricky hedger, thatcher of solid name,
The fiery preacher, tireless sifter of truth.

His liver had killed him next year when I came.
The house was sold and the mares, the pleasant holding
Falling to fallow, his fame thinning to dream.

Already he was recalled as mean, and lusting
For girls and sugar, a hypocrite, dying boasting.

SNOW IN LONDON

All day from the east slanted snow
Covering pavement toys and the metal men
Who speak for England the lead laws of ago.

The ugly and the best-unseen were strewn
With white's illusion, and the brittle clocks
Cracked in the silence of an air of stone.

Rank through the noon was smell of beeves and cocks
Slain for the Child and gleaming in the eye
Like fishes nestling in the island rocks.

Beauty was white but poor man's bitter day
To tempt the tongue and soak the thinning shoe
That walks to heaven by the neon way.

Griming the white of time's unstable floe,
Man's shame survived the judgements of the snow.

THE TRAMP

Dirtying the joy of the returning exile
At the hemlock lane falling from the crest,
He rises like conscience or the paternal call.

Lolling face, tufted by tangled waste,
Round as balloon painted with mouth and eyes,
Deflates a grin above a woolen chest.

Negroid lips split and eyes glitter two ways,
The paint becomes alive, like blood under dirt,
The rubber features vivify with menace,

And tell the story of the mountain chart
Fastened to the otherwise worthless will
And the search postponed by an unstable heart.

Then, promising gold from the eventual spoil,
Takes conscientious pence and limps downhill.

MERTHYRMAWR

Sunday evening. The thick-lipped men binoculared
Steal through the geometric groves of pines
Observing the steady and fatal hands of poachers
And the young loving in wrinkles of the dunes.

Grey in the wind sand tides against the turrets,
And watchful sight is bridged towards the sea,
Where silent the marram defends a wearing land
And the seagulls climb like Junkers a plaster sky.

The air is alive with voices, the loving whisper,
The rodent scream at neck-constricting hand,
Gulls' earthless wail and dank watchers' laughter.
Always the wind whistles through teeth of sand.

Night falls on the lovers, marram and voices.
Dark hinders eyes, yet aids the brutal hand.
Watchers depart, but the snares are filling.
Wind dries the blood on the moving sand.

THAMES

The punts are laid up for a profitless summer;
Anadyomene, the virgins shimmer
Rising from the backwater, sunburnt and slimmer.

Fungoid in the meadows tents are built.
The trains are full, and by the riparian halt
Their wheels crush out the detected master's guilt.

All weirs are dry, and foetid cords of slime
Drip from their steps to pools undashed by foam.
The anglers are playful; the virgins without shame.

And in the evenings the gramophones
Sing through the clotting dusk in metal tones
The amorous laments of stones and towns.

The anglers boast of escapades on cliffs.
Under the branches, from the swaying skiffs
Are heard the virgins' protests and the throaty laughs.

SUMMER FIRE

Flowing across the shrivelled grass
The fire runs from the railway line
Into the orchard, ringing the cherry trees
With hounds of fire.

Where the fire has passed
A carpet of sable;
Brown and withered the cherry leaves.

ROSES AND CHRISTMAS ROSES

I saw white roses on Christmas morning,
white buds of tight rose ivory,
never wide-blooming, never revealing their fullness
of intimate stamen gold
to grey cold winter skies.

And in the shadow of the same rose briar
white moon cups, stars
of clotted snow,
upborne
on shafts of green pale ice,
sun-avoiding,
in the shadow
coldly born and consummated.

WINTER WHEAT

The blue rosettes of winter wheat
form ranks in the yellow clay.
Their tarnished swords
are spread with sharp antagonism
in a barbed circle protecting their identity,
uncompromising selfness.
But they will grow,
washed by the rain of spring,
into tall slender brothers
leaning together,
whispering in gentle voices.

SAWMILL

No tenor droning of the circular saw,
snort of donkey engine,
purr of belt over slotted wheels,
clatter of new planks stacked,
crunch of tires on the gravel,
no hoarse voices of men . . .

But black buildings stacked against the sky,
the dereliction of a rusting engine,
a tramp's fire winking behind abandoned cordwood . . .

READING TOLSTOY

Now Levin drinks the water flecked with rust
And in my mouth a bitter tang of iron
Draws flat. Rabbits lived then; their sandy warren
Grew mushrooms big as plates; dark in own dusk
The oakwood clambered down its red soft cliff
And stuck its feet of alder deep in bog.
In that sour sedge once woodcocks came to dig
With long pronged totem bills and stiff
Steps angular. They fled in lumbering zigzags.
Whether I saw those rare dark namesake birds,
As once bright hoopoe high on Alpine road,
Or made a myth from small snipes' stilted legs,
I know no more. But see the marsh return,
The birds in problem shadows strutting, brass
Blaring of kingcups down the dank morass,
And dense beneath the cliff a nest of fern
Where crystal out of green the spring jets forth
And fills the small tin cup whose taste wakes in my mouth.

FIRST SPRING ON THE ISLAND

Our first spring on that island. Other strangers
Had prospered there, but now the land was sick,
Worked out and overgrown with broom and alder.
Still, every day, alone, I'd take the track
Down from the trailer in among the firs
And hack down broom.   Broom petals, winter honey,
Dripped on my sweaty arms. The limping killdeer
Cried through the grass in wing-drag mockery
And garter snakes whipped sliding brown from blade
Beyond death's accident—till in that knot
Of blue-eyed grass one turned to coil and sway,
Struck venomless and bit upon my boot,
That small head jabbing vainly at its hardness.
I held death's poisoned fang that day. I struck
With rage and loathing, struck again, again—
Most madly mashed his body with my stick
And dropped its pulp among the sky-tinged flowers.
Twelve years ago, but deathless in the brain,
A snake's strange courage, and my human shame.

IV.

DEATH AND THE DISTANT PRINCESS

Death and the Maiden—the perennial romantic combination— is a category that can sweep in a great number of vaguely related works in any poet's repertory. In fact, the preceding sections have already included poems that concern death in other contexts; here it appears either on its own or in combination with love. Love in its turn appears most often in combination with the idea of distance, of parting, even of meetings never achieved, and in this sense distance becomes a little death. Reading these poems leads me to the conclusion that—for me at least—it has rarely been deep and lasting experiences or relationships that have moved me to expression in verse. To live them has been sufficient. It is more often the accidental relationship, the fleeting contact complicated by parting, by one's very sense of evanescence, that for me has been conducive to poetry. And here I think one returns inevitably to George Orwell's remark, in his essay on Dickens, that "A writer's literary personality has little or nothing to do with his private character." Certainly in poetry I have found that to be true. One seizes, in other words, on the incidents and circumstances in one's life that can be transformed into myth. To give only one example, let me cite the references to Provençal place names contained in the poems of this section; I had been in Provence briefly not many months before World War II began in 1939, and during the six years of isolation from Europe that followed, the images of that stark, brilliant and history-encrusted region represented for me all that was denied; hence, "Song for the South" and similar poems. A less striking place, in which I had lived longer and been more genuinely happy, would not have provided such images, which had value precisely because of their exotic and unfamiliar nature.

SONG FOR THE SOUTH

Beyond the islands where my knees are set
In solitary snow, in rock and ice,
Lay out your South in sands of wine and heat,
In hills of drowsy hands and sad olive trees.

Surrender so all ripeness of your fruit,
Pomegranate-coloured warmth, down youth on peach,
Purple of pulp, the intricate flowering sweet
Soft fig pouting to the greedy reach.

Be in mind's Avignon the dropping night,
Winter where swallows are immune from frost,
And where mnemonic artifices shout
The inarticulate blood within your breast.

So from your heart let the slow stalks of ease
Bind round my solitude the briar of peace.

NOW

Now I compare the forecasts with events,
Noting the lucky prophecy of each seer,
It is no calm of courage in the spring
That has outdriven my autumn fear.

It is no certainty of hiding safe
From steel or the conscripting hand of death
Swells my eternity like a tube of peace
Lipped to the wet staunchness of the earth.

Only the pattern of your wishing parts
Me so from fate. I cannot be afraid,
Though unheroic, when the nightmare gods
Pass dangerously as sniping flight of lead.

You are invisible friendship in this forest,
Warning the shadows and the bladder ogres;
You are the solid hand driving from highways
Talking ghosts and cannibal women-fakers.

You, speaking and silent with me, and loved
Here and away, make Now a lucky land
Where the electric walls bar fear's black hour
And many flowers turn gold from the happy hand.

But Now, authentic Phoenix, dies as lives.
Now lasts only as instant. Now is land
Where the events are, Now is not event.
And when the events attack, what walls shall stand?

AIGUES MORTES

Earth is the town that squares my eye
And out of salt the strength of bone
Builds the citadel high and high
Over the gardens growing stone.

Into stone the faces grow.
The pectoral contours set in rock.
Heat burns the heart as dead as snow
And beauty sleeps like shells in chalk.

Salt on the eyelid and the lip
Tortures the flesh too tired for tears.
The visions into marshes slip,
Sink and are lost beneath their fears,
And in such land of mire and stone
Your absence withers all my green.

INSULAR POEM

Cast on your beaches, whose flexed currents throw
Men and thoughts as brash, I rise and view
Your island face, whose tides without moon
Make palms mirage and valleys without sun.

Those like Gerbault who escaped by sails
Or sought the unknown Alpine above hills
Leave I lonely distance when I dare
Black and thicket jungle of your hair.

And drawn by soil magnetic of your mouth,
As sailors going native in the south
Burn their clothes and photographs of home,
I let tides gulf all craft wherewith I come.

Till, exile and expatriate for you,
Cut from all past by love's marooning flow,
I am Selkirk standing on the only island
Or last man on the last submerging strand.

THE FOUNTAIN AT VAUCLUSE

Many years in sentimental willing exile
Petrarch walked beside the inky waters,
Posing the gentle rebel and inconsolable lover,
Expecting laurels and extolling Laura
In the sickly voice of an emotion long dead.

Meanwhile, in Avignon, married and virtuous,
Laura had brats, grew matronly and fat,
And worshipped strictly under the Papal shadow.
She hardly thought of Petrarch beside the inky waters,
And died respected for every homely virtue.

After her death he left the enigmatic waters
And returned to the jaded valley at Avignon,
Where, under the Papal shadow and the cicada,
The laurels fell on his lined and lofty brow.

MEMORANDUM FROM ARCADIA

I in Arcadia lived. I have traced on stone
   The record of cold days, and scratched on glass
   The seismograph's stutter (Time would erase
Figures on paper or iron, would rot even bone).

For hunters I have shown the tracks of deer
   With bent boughs, cairns and tablets nailed on trees.
   I have marked the levels of the inland seas,
And watched the salmon courting at each weir,

I have experimented with foodstuffs, eaten snails
   And nettles (finding the latter tough).
   I have found the water clear and tasty enough.
I have kept the wolves from the hut with wooden rails.

Explorers who follow me into the hut will find
   Blankets and sheets, matches on the table,
   Tins of food, a wrecked launch's cable,
A telephone directory, a white stick for the blind.

I shall do the thing the neatest and cleanest way.
   Cord rots soon. I shall drop to the floor.
   I shall be found behind the kitchen door
Sprawling untidily on the trodden clay.

WINDOWS

Windows from which the captains stepped to death,
Climbing from time on condemnation's tear,
Borne on the breath of boys beyond their fear,
Above illusion and hate's human heat;

Windows at which the girls left life for love,
Stepping in joy to indecisive fate;
Windows at which the burning sang too late
To shun the end death's salamanders live;

All windows open in those fluid ports
That are your eyes, where shadow armies roll
Constricted in destruction, rulers fall
Like walls in earthquake, all ambitions wane
As in Les Baux the fig trees break and part
The dying town where grass seeps in again.

POEM FOR GARCIA LORCA

Count on dead fingers of time the years that pass
Since Lorca sang his last of Spain
And fell beneath the hard inhuman paw,
Gasping between white walls in Granada.

Lorca, the song of men whose emptying hearts
Sang out the seconds of their death in blood,
The song of women whose bloodless futures lay
Twisted under the roof of tyranny.

Remember Lorca as Spain's noblest bull,
Not in the sunlight of Mithraic rings
Spurting his life to matadors and crowds
But in numb secrecy to the knacker's laugh.

Remember Lorca as the earth of Spain,
Lined with valleys as an old man's hand,
In each valley the gun lurking and the dead waiting
For the dawn that will not break their empty sleep.

Remember Lorca as the poor of Spain,
Rising once from their alleys of quiet death
To wash with blood the roots of barren trees
That do not bloom this year and one year will fall for ever.

Remember Lorca, who died only for being Lorca.

BATTLE OF BRITAIN

A fakir's rope of smoke hooked in the sky
    Marks the copse that shags the facing hill,
The burnt angles tangling the trees in steel
    And the banks of cyclists building a motley wall.

A stumbling cortege reaches the chilly sun
    Trampling a slow path through the kneeing grain.
The bundle in their arms is the aviator,
    Shrouded in coats his locked face of pain.

He was young. He will burn again
    Vicariously in dreams. The smoke thins into blue.
Cyclists return to their tandems. On the heath
    Swivel and roar the yapping snouts of guns.

SOLITARY

Time gutters like a leaking tap
On lonely waiting for the 'phones to ring
In one-rooms of home where gas taps wait
For tired fingers to loose Lethe like song.

And I am with those solitary in small hells,
Watching their acts as if my shadow moved,
Knowing in them the glasses of a life
When without you my life too shall have died.

For all is potential in us: boredom and fear,
The undefeatable dread of naked selves,
And hope surviving, tenuous, to the hour
When the hand turning inward ends and saves.

A FARMER'S EPITAPH

Deep night upholds the heavy doom
Of roses over Shepherd's tomb,
And he who tore the acres lies
Where brain knows no Spring ecstacies.
In six by two of blue-green clay
Earth has her still revenge today.

V.

THE END MAN

If my anarchist faith fostered in me the sense of regeneration arising from destruction, as in Bakunin's celebrated aphorism, there was also a naturally pessimistic side to my mind that believed man was—perhaps deservedly—doomed. In part, I may have been influenced by Eliot and other pessimistic writers of the Twenties, but I believe it was a temperamental strain in my own nature that made me catch the resonances of poems like "The Hollow Men". Certainly I was not thinking of Eliot when I wrote the poems of this section. At the end of the Thirties when the shadow of war hung over us, and at the end of the war when it looked as though the world would continue in its old bad way, I saw man either dying out ignominiously, or pursued by unnamed furies of his own creation, as in "Ballad of the End Man" and "The Tower", to an end without dignity. I cannot say that at that time I had reasoned out the kind of scenario which the prophets of ecological doom have recently presented, for one side of me still failed to criticize the optimistic socialist beliefs that the goods of the earth were unlimited, but I did seriously consider even then, as I still do, that man may be an evolutionary failure and on his way to join the dinosaurs, whom he so resembles in the imbalance of his development. A sense of the inevitability and unfairness of personal death was balanced by a sense of the inevitability and perhaps the justice of the death of the species, collective man having betrayed individual man. These poems have to be placed with the "Anarchist Elegies" to complete a divided vision.

BALLAD OF THE END MAN

On that day skeletons from all cupboards
Emerged, shouting the past, pointing the derogatory finger.

Among ghosts also the rising was universal,
Not one keeping his post to guard an evil tradition.

The rulers were nonplussed by this insurrection,
For the dead were immune from poison gas or gun.

At eight o'clock the massacre began,
The slaughter of the living by guilt and confusion.

Some went mad. Some stood their ground. Most fled
Into the last wild woods along the marches.

Nestlings and still-born lambs became our foods,
Our houses piles of boulders thatched with reeds,

While the victorious rioted in our homes,
Eating the Oxford Marmalade, lapping the wines.

For us there was no rest in our misfortune,
No sanctuary immune from death's deathless vision.

And one by one they have found each hiding place
And wormed out the hidden. I am the last of my race.

So spoke the end man, as he became a ghost,
Received in triumph by the spectral host.

THE LAST MAN

There is an only challenger to his kingdom.
Through the faint ruin of paddy field and vine
The last man, conscious of finality,
Climbs, carrying history like a shell.

Slow is the hour when, Selkirk of a world,
His lonely mind surveys a fragment realm
Of manless cities where the rats remain.
The remnants of his reign, the iron toys
Left from the past, shine with the perished eyes
Of his deciduous comrades. Theirs his end
Waits on the mountain with his only foe,
The shadow that will smile and be himself
When falls his ash to the residual us
As Arctic time assaults the senile world.

SONG

Time's destroying claws
Scatter sand and soil,
Crush the seed and the bulb,
But in brain's damp earth
Memory evades the dog.

So our thought has still
Beauty grudging smiles,
Deeds boy heroes did,
Anger and the thin
Residue left by death.

And as skeleton leaves
Live again in frost
We shall keep for age
Folly and bitterness
And disillusion's itch.

THE GREEN MOAT OF TIME

Time, a green moat around the castled mind,
Holds corpses in its depth, that rise and sink
On tides of thought, stirred by the blind
Currents among the weeded shadows of the brink.

Bound hand and foot, their bloated bodies float
Sometimes under battlements where the watcher stands;
Their eyes are eaten by fishes, their grey cheeks wet
With slime where their hair creeps in weedy strands.

Yet in those dead features the watcher sees
A moment live across the wasted faces,
When the lips become red and vanished eyeballs rise
And the swollen tongue speaks thickly and accuses.

And as such bodied memories sink and fade,
Leaving their ripples on the closing slime,
The watcher turns within the walls, to hide
His dread of failure and his fear of time.

THE TOWER

Last night the sappers halted. Under my house
Their tapping ceased. The silence deafened with fear
As I saw through earth the shifting eye of the fuse.

As timed the mine's jet rose. In the explosion
Seven died. But I, the sought man, fled
Into the hills, this roofless tower's seclusion.

Babel above me, to the metallic sky
Stone funnels. Gaps in the crumbling wall
Show the peaceful village and the cold sea.

The hovels are stone, warm when night is dry.
Matted thistles uphold the caving thatch
And sheeted iron denotes prosperity.

Here seems no gold of sun or coin to seek,
No prey or promise for owl or limping fox,
But gain only for the man needing peace.

Yet the prophetic sounds in my brain domed
Expand to fill the quiet of the sky
With the tap in the tunnel and the winged hum.

For here, I know, my enemies' saps will creep,
Pushed to explosive ends, and to new dens
I shall restage the skin-of-teeth escape.

Time and again I shall repeat the act,
Fear and relief and fear, as every hour
March the soulless figures of the zodiac clock.

DOOMED HABITATIONS

Looking into the windows that doom has broken
Where the vague star illumines death and dust
And the shadows of actions whose ends are forsaken
Stir under the falling walls, senile and lost,

And looking into the doorways where unspoken names
Shine and disintegrate on the rotting plaques,
Surviving their owners who have left like dreams,
Sinking into the past as sea-sucked wrecks.

Remember, stranger, that here men grew and worked,
Loved and were angry, and in general lived
Peaceable lives till one day, spitted on their brothers' knives,
Stuck to the curdling heart by nails they loved,
They died in horror and their towns were left,
And rotted, buried under the dust and leaves.

TO SIMONE SAINT-SABIN AT SACRÉ COEUR, 1938

One day when fallen are these icy domes
That mock Byzantium, and this teeming hill's
Land for the plough like Carthage, spades will come
Proving like surgeons under the sheep's kale.

And in the tin museum among the folds
Stooping archaeologists with black beards
Will piece the glasses found in the Rue Pigalle,
Index the wine corks and the visiting cards.

If I can stand then under this white wall
I shall see your looks fall over vanished Paris
As you tell your old tale of the Virgin and her roses,
Ignoring the Commune and its wall's blood of many.

I shall also hear you shout in another hour:
"I would stand behind a mitrailleuse for France!"
And wonder at you and that lost love of land
Whose verbal glory spelt with dots from guns.

CAUGHT ON THE HOP

Mercury ebbs in the sterile tubes
   When Death, the god with the eyeless socket,
   With ice in his heart and fire in his pocket,
Enters and fuses the wires and the bulbs.

The rats and the birds on the telegraph wires
   Saw his arrival and made their escape.
   But we who were watching the news on the tape
Saw not the lights dim or sinking fires.

We're caught on the hop—too late to depart.
   Death, with his knives and his satchels of bombs
   Opens the doors and strides through the rooms
With fire in his pocket and ice in his heart.

AT THIS HOUR

Record that at this hour decisions are made
Whether to plant the dragon in the shade,
Whether to write or let the offer slide,
Whether to breed, and who shall be the bride?

Record that cricketers are shedding pads
As farmers scatter their last rain of seeds,
And in the hills the clouds are signed with red
For men to die after the ore has bled.

Record that flanges are straining at the rail
And planes are eager to shed their monstrous hail,
The wolf is waiting and the worm in egg
Grows for the Attic face and runner's leg.

THE BONES OF LOVE

Who can record the street's temptation?
I crush the dry bones underfoot
And the devil's instruction bubbles through blood.
The word is annihilation.

We burn as children die in arms.
The devil's word within our hearts
Whirls in a gyroscope of fire.
The dry bones break in many forms.

The stones reject the foot of love.
The devil's gospel in the stones
Breaks the age and breaks the bones.
Day's eyelid closes on the grave.

SPOKEN IN LOVE

Spoken in love, no new vernacular
Rises this season from the heart
Through the breaking images, the secular
Figures of toil or sport.

Love in this season, as unicorn fabulous
Feeds in countries far away.
Under the passionate heart and the sedulous
Manner the heart is clay.

So in this spring when canker autumnal
Lies as seed in the breaking bud
Deeds are sterile and ice perpetual
Sets pain in the slow blood.

SPEECH FROM THE DOCK

You who of empty worlds are denizen,
Livers in time who sleep in broken hell,
Or speak the dying languages of pain,
You whom the burning hours transmit no bell;

And you whose far and lovely fatherland
Lives beyond future and the final star,
Whose battling journeys tell no happy end
Seen in horizons where the ideal are;

As on this bitter breath of night we ride
Across a time we cannot turn away
Into a spurious past or future burning red,
I ask you—forget your dreams and live today.

No clock, once turned, ticks the same hour again,
No time runs straight the route of our desire.
Our yearnings to the past are calls in vain;
Towards no future can our charts be sure.

It is only in now our hope can ever live,
Where past and future are absorbed and blent.
Only in now the sick can ever love
And the lost art achieve its orient.

VI.

NEW POEMS

These are the most recent poems, written over the last winter, and too close for me to see them in the temporal perspective through which I have been viewing my earlier works. All I can say of most of them at present is contained in "Prologue". However, I should perhaps point out that while many of these poems are written in a freer form than I habitually used in the past, I have deliberately returned in a few cases to regular forms, partly led by the desire to prove, after so long, that certain technical skills have not vanished, but partly also because I believe that traditional fixed poetic forms still have their uses, especially when they are combined with the devices of parody or deliberate pastiche.

PROLOGUE

Remembering
Hardy and Yeats
singing again
in the last years
I knew
muteness would end.
Survival was all.

I thought
singing again
I would celebrate
living things,
birds
and animals whom I prefer
mostly to men,
the green earth
that renews my mind,
and those instants
epiphanous
when the light
transfigures a landscape
and transvalues.

Yet now
my voice hurries
down the green valleys,
between the incandescent mountains,
and under the sonorous clouds
of swirling snow geese,
jays, gulls and eagles,

ignoring them all
to sing of death
and the dark love
that grows in
death's dark shadow
like the purple blossom
of soldanella
thawing its way
up through the radiant
snow.

VICTORIAN CUSTOM

Grasping the barrel,
within season of course,
you pulled a shotgun,
loaded and cocked
through a quick hedge,
across a stone fence.
A thorn
or a rock edge
tipped the trigger,
blew your side in.
It was almost a
Victorian custom.
Speke of the Nile
did it
to avoid facing Burton,
and my great-grandfather,
Thomas Woodcock,
to avoid facing
a roomful of daughters
without dowries.

Juries of sportsmen
returned appropriate verdicts.
They knew
in those days
that life also
is mainly accidental.

THE GAME SHOP IN COLMAR

The shop front is Art Nouveau,
drab green, with the word GIBIER
gold on a foxed mirror,
and iron hooks welded
to an iron bar
over the window.
Draggled bunches of hares
and pheasants
hang limp as rags,
so unlike themselves
that I forget the buck hare
I watched with joy last night
on a moonlit road's edge,
cavorting among the cabbages;
forget him, and think I'll enjoy
for dinner tonight
a *hasenpfeffer,* piquant, hot.

Think, that is, until I see
those dark eyes
staring
out of the shop's depth.

The doe's head
rests on a chopping block,
but the eyes are still so bright
and sorrowful
that at first I think it a live beast,
and then, peering in,
see the severed cylinder
of brown neck
behind the alert eyes.

There is something
invincibly
human about
decapitation.
No animal can perform
such tidy severance.
I think at once
of Mary Queen of Scots
and Anne Bullen,
wondering if their eyes
looked with the same hopeless reproach
at the henchmen and headsmen
of the fierce Tudors.

Then mind flips
twenty years,
five thousand miles,
arid Guanajuato, the catacombs
whose desiccated dead
lounge in the attitudes of
an interrupted and consequently
eternal debauch,
when they are not lying in their coffins,
paralysed in the last struggle,
mouths shouting silence,
arms resisting air,
no gentle goers
into any night.
I watch them
with a defensive irony
until at the feet of these
roisterers and resisters
my eye freezes
on a head that looks severed;
no body,
a swathe of black hair
and a tight mask of features,

lips retracted, empty sockets.
Young once, perhaps lovely,
like the doe in the gameshop
staring at me.

And as mind flips back
doe and dead woman
are one,
and the iron hooks
creak under Gestapo game,
echt menschenfleisch,
wingless and two-legged
whitemeat.

Tonight, for dinner,
I eat fish.
Their blood is cold,
their eyes are coloured discs,
expressionless,
without depth
or reproach.
Even the Buddhist monks
in Thailand
eat them
without sense of sin.

REVISIONIST LEGEND ONE

I do not know
who was Jocasta's
father (though that
would be easy to find)
but seeing you,
untouched by your own hand
mourning Oedipus
who broke the legend
(dying before you
and unblinded),
I look into your doe's
dark hunted eyes
and being, as they say,
quite old enough to be
your father, I imagine
how Jocasta's father
loved his daughter,
and suspecting that the phoenix
to stir up trouble
gave the wrong answers,
I am drained with sadness
until the sparkling tears
waken your eyes,
provoke my longing.

REVISIONIST LEGEND TWO

I let you down, of course,
doubly, watching
your heels kick at the
tipped-up stool, but
staying alive, and also
unblinded, even
unblinkered.   It has been
clarification and
a freeing.

Remember, I was the ignorant
coming in off the road
with blood on my hands.
You, having heard the
prophecy, knew and savoured
revenge's rankness, when that
self-grown instrument which
fate returned
both killed and cuckolded
your enemy, my father.

There were always tears.   Ours
was a necessary union, destined
not happy,
from the moment you
designed dementia
in palace corridors and
I came upon you, weeping and
naked, wandering.

There was more afterwards
when I turned to the young ones.
Jabbed by jealousy
the ghost then
rose in your nightmare.
There was struggle
at the barred doors, shouting
of river and rope,
and guards gossiping
in the town.

One day, even
in the interests of state,
it was inevitable
my hand should cease
restraining.
If letting die is
murder,
I am your murderer;
if upsetting the prophecy
is hubris
the gods are my enemies.

But, unblinding myself, I
see the deities in their
chthonian burrows
as earth,
necessity from which we
rise—and above!

Letting unreason die
makes reason triumph;
one becomes oneself by
renewing the
father murdered, and
one's realm is
undivided
until the next
cycle begins ·
below
    Delphi
        at the
           crossroads.

ELEGY ON ARCHERS

The archer stood, alone,
in the Indian cemetary
at Kitwancool, and unique.
No other Tsimshian carving
resembled that lithe
renaissance vision
poised on his column,
the stringless bow
directed skyward
and the whole figure
bronzed with lichen,
made ethereal
by wood's decay.
Who carved him, and why,
in a village of solid
and sombre totems, nobody knew.
Long fallen, he has rotted
into the long grasses
by the sullen river,
yet loiters
in the dark of my memory
to return as your image,
sibling or double.

For you too practiced
that beautiful and archaic
art of accuracy
and destruction
and other arts of stark
and calligraphic beauty.
How far you understood
object and implication
of such hieratic modes
I never knew,
and yet you stand
in memory framed in them,
in figure like the vanished
archer of melting wood,
your bow sky-lifted,
your arrow drawn and driven
into the light
by which you lived
in which you die.

very intellectual poetry
late interest in mythic figures

SILENT HOUNDS LOPING

The night
drifts into your forest
and the cry
grows faint.
The hounds are silent
loping towards you,
old hunter, dying.

Seeing another forest
where the hounds waited,
hunter and warrior
tonight you weep;
with old man's tears
wash time away.
A lost front, a lost war,
drowned under six decades of history
rises to you out of memory.

We stand beside you
under the pine trees
and the night waits
for chance to speak,
the enemy unseen.
You, and that boy you see
with such choking memory,
crawl through the heath and fern
into the night
that breaks with noise and light.
Then through the light he falls
in night for ever

and you
hacked deep by lead
survive to nurse your wounds
and not forget.
Holding your hand
in the instant of hallucination
I become your comrade.
You weep for me also.

Old mountaineer
you stand
at the white saddle
on your way down
from the blinding peak
where you have seen
guides and companions
fall past you into space,
you helpless.
It is all memory
but for you as real
as your delirium
and for us as real
as your tears falling
bright as if frozen
into the dark crevasse
where the men you survive
and the beasts you slaughtered
wait.

THE GEOMANTIC DRAGON

Turning black mould
under the oak tree
in the garden's corner
where we had dug
often
and found nothing
it was you encountered
the dragon.

From a great vessel
by dead fingers made,
a splinter sharp as a knife,
and as we washed
the lines
faint and cerulean
emerged out of greyness,
Chinese cloud arcs
and sailing through them
the magic reptile,
wings, tail and horns
complete, fire-breathing
self- magnifying.

Was this the being,
true landlord, lord of lands,
protector geomantic
who rang clear bells
in old house corners
and when we worked
through the night's depth
sent odour of violets,
cakes and stables
seeping fresh
from place's past,
benevolent?

Was this he,
tired of speaking
to ear and nostril,
taking new form
to offer through eye
and fingertip
validation of our life,
and the best years of a lifetime
spent in this garden,
green well of shadow,
under the giant cherry
whose eighty years' abundance
feeds wasps and robins,
flickers, raccoons
and other friends
less animal and wise,
and white enclouds
in spring
the house you also
discovered
on your first meeting—
unaware then—
with the dragon
who compelled our choice
and now offers
his image in blue lines
on the fragment of a vessel
made by some old Chinese,
eye and hand wise
and, like yourself,
shaper of forms,
a potter?

Dragon king
of unknown provenance,
unexpected arrival
and undoubted
Taoist allegiance,
accept this invocation,
bless our life
within your guarded land
with love and
dragon's gifts,
the power to change,
to grow in the
fluidity transforming
eternal dark to light.

BALLAD FOR W.H. AUDEN

As I walked out one evening,
   Walking down Granville Street,
The fog drained off the mountains
   And the air blew wet with sleet.

And there you walked beside me
   In the desert of my thought,
With your lost ambiguous brilliance
   And the wit time set at naught.

The glass was dark in your mirror.
   You held it. I looked in pain.
In that face turned lunar landscape
   I saw the earth of Spain.

I saw the arid valleys
   Where the quick and the dead still wait,
And I knew why your answer was silence
   And how silence shaped your fate.

I walked down Granville with Spender
   In a different, golden year,
And Spender said: "God and Auden,
   They call each other Dear!"

O master of my awakening
   Who made me hear aright,
O leader lost of my twenties
   Who elected for faith and flight,

O patient and private poet,
   Who blessed each hovering day
With prayer and vision and practice
   Both God-directed and lay,

And in the American desert
    Kept your Lent and your craft intact,
My mind makes me turn and salute you
    And life as an artifact.

But my eyes look in your mirror,
    I see the rived image it shows,
And my heart speaks out in answer,
    And my desperation grows,

For what the glass has awakened
    Is neither envy nor joy
But the pity I felt at your passing
    By so narrow and wearing a way.

Yet your image speaks like a judgment
    As if your body declared,
"Let me accept the sentence,
    And my brother soul be spared!"

If your Anglican God has received you
    As Auden or Wystan or Dear,
I know that all is accepted
    With irony, without fear,

As the fog drains off the mountains
    And the air blows wet with sleet,
Walking ghostly out one evening,
    Walking down Granville Street.

PAPER ANARCHIST ADDRESSES THE SHADE
OF NANCY LING PERRY

Out of our daylight into death you burn,
　　For words once lit you, sparks struck out of books,
And as you char to memory I learn
　　How words life-tempered bend to cruel hooks.

Among those words perhaps some were my own,
　　Written within the fiery coil of youth,
When ambiguity was left unknown
　　And consequences seemed no bar to truth:

Truth as then seen, sharp white and shadow black,
　　And as you saw it, leading through flame's dawn,
　　　The only causes time and fear and place
Why you, not I, enter that violent dark
　　And I look on, appalled, ashamed, and mourn
　　　Terrible children, comrades, enemies.

BINARIES

1

"We are all lonely," you said
at dreamtime out of death,
from which I must conclude
that being dead
is as private a matter
as dying
or living.

2

Lady believe
your sixteen summers bracing at the blouse
too tight for blowsiness,
that old man's look of rage
is lust not anger,
is lust's despair, not love.

3

Soul, clap your hands,
    But do not sing;
Your angel flies
    On raven wing.

ON COMPLETING A LIFE OF DUMONT

who is Dumont
ask Peter

A year I have lived in the most of my mind with you,
Acting your deeds as best I can, thinking your thoughts, and
Now I stand back, take your dark presence in my view,
And realize that though we say goodbye, easy hand
In hand, like companions ending a long hard journey,
We are still strangers, you from your world where
Violence is what happens in the natural daily way
Between animals and between men, I from the rare
Interlude of a time where peace has been a fragile
Possibility in a few favoured places for a few.
But what is the echo I hear compellingly ring
In my ear as you bow sardonically into your defile
Of dark death?   What does it tell me I share with you?
Is it, fierce stranger, that freedom is a word our hearts both sing?

NOTES ON VISITATIONS

Sometimes
when I am alone
the music strikes
and I sing
with confidence and ease
the increasingly complex
melodies
of Mozart's
never lived
and final years.

Or the rhythm
enters my limbs
and I step
like a Greek sailor,
companion of Odysseus,
prancing with
elephantine joyful
solemnity and without
benefit of choreography
between my books,   my
manuscripts piled high
as obsolescent
obstacles
to dancing.

Or I am seized
with glossolaliac
motions
and the verses
stutter out
in metric order
and a new tongue,
unknown yet obvious
with meaning.
This occurs
walking in woods.

But always
when the fit strikes
I am alone,
walls down, gates
open and always
the pending onrush
of joy
lifts into ecstacy
of limbs
gyrating
or tumbling
unsilenceable
voice.

Such visitations
possessed me at sixteen,
and at sixty
the gods
revisit.